Arron's L

A collection of poetry by Arron Waters with photography by Stephen Treharne

Cefnogi Pobl a Chymunedau | Supporting People and Communities

Published by Iconau
Glan Morfa
Ferryside
SA17 5TF
iconau.com

First published 2021
© Arron Waters
© Stephen Treharne
All rights reserved

ISBN 978-1-907476-34-1

edited by Stephen Treharne
cover design: from the Welsh Writing Desk
original illustration: jazegraphics@hotmail.com
typeset in Arial: write4word.org
printed: proprint-wales.co.uk

British Library Cataloguing in Publication data
A cataloguing record for this book is available from the British
Library.

The Taste of Ice Cream

Arron's Lockdown

I bawb yng Nghwmni Cartrefi Cymru Cooperative am eu dewrder, eu tosturi, eu dygnwch, a'u creadigrwydd yn ystod pandemig Covid yn 2020/21

To everyone at Cartrefi Cymru Co-operative for their bravery, compassion, endurance and creativity during the Covid pandemic of 2020/21

Rhagair

Mae pandemig Covid wedi bod yn gyfnod anodd i bawb ledled y byd. Daeth pethau yr oeddem i gyd yn eu cymryd yn ganiataol, fel gallu ymweld â lleoedd a chwrdd â phobl, i gyd i stop. Roedd yn rhaid i ni ddod i arfer â dilyn llawer o reolau a dod o hyd i ffyrdd newydd o fyw a gweithio.

Mae wedi bod yn arbennig o anodd i bobl ag anghenion iechyd a gofal. Cawsant eu torri i ffwrdd yn sydyn oddi wrth eu teulu a'u ffrindiau ac yn aml roeddent yn cael trafferth deall beth oedd yn digwydd. Mae hefyd wedi bod yn her enfawr i'r staff rheng flaen a oedd yn gorfod cadw pobl yn ddiogel ac yn iach wrth roi eu hunain mewn perygl bob diwrnod gwaith. Mae wedi bod yn gyfnod a ddaeth â'r gorau mewn pobl a meithrin bondiau cryf rhwng y rhai sy'n derbyn cefnogaeth a'r rhai sy'n ei ddarparu.

Mae'r llyfr hwn yn dathlu'r berthynas rhwng dau berson o'r fath, Arron Waters a'i weithiwr cymorth Stephen Treharne. Gyda'i gilydd maent wedi cyd-gynhyrchu gwaith o eiriau a lluniau sy'n cyfleu rhwystredigaethau'r pandemig ar ei anterth, a phleserau dychwelyd i rywbeth fel normalrwydd.

Foreword

The Covid pandemic has been a difficult time for everyone all over the world. Things that we all took for granted, like being able to visit places and meet people, all came to a stop. We had to get used to following lots of rules and find new ways of living and working.

It has been especially difficult for people with health and care needs. They were suddenly cut off from their family and friends and often struggled to understand what was going on. It has also been a massive challenge for the frontline staff who had to keep people safe and well whilst putting themselves at risk every working day. It has been a time that brought out the best in people and forged strong bonds between those receiving support and those providing it.

This book celebrates the relationship between two such people, Arron Waters and his support worker Stephen Treharne. Together they have co-produced a work of words and pictures that brilliantly captures the frustrations of the pandemic at its height, and the pleasures of a return to something like normality.

Ledled Cymru, mae pobl fel Arron a Stephen wedi rhannu eu rhwystredigaethau gyda'i gilydd ac wedi dod o hyd i ffyrdd creadigol o lenwi diwrnodau hir o unigedd gyda pha bynnag gelf a chrefft y gallent droi eu llaw atynt. Fe allech chi lenwi amgueddfa gyda'r holl waith celf a barddoniaeth a gynhyrchwyd yn ystod Covid gan staff Cartrefi a'r bobl maen nhw'n eu cefnogi. Mae'r llyfr hwn wedi'i gyflwyno iddyn nhw i gyd, ond gyda diolch arbennig i Arron a Stephen am roi ffordd mor wych i ni gofio a dathlu.

Adrian Roper
Prif Swyddog Gweithredol, Cartrefi Cymru Co-operative

All over Wales, people like Arron and Stephen have shared their frustrations together and found creative ways of filling long days of isolation with whatever arts and crafts they could turn their hand to. You could fill a museum with all the artwork and poetry produced during Covid by Cartrefi staff and the people they support. This book is dedicated to them all, but with especial thanks to Arron and Stephen for giving us such a great way of remembering and celebrating.

Adrian Roper
CEO, Cartrefi Cymru Co-operative

Contents

Part 1: Lockdowns

Part 2: 2021

Part 1
Lockdowns

Hat on the Wall

I don't like this hat really
my head gets warm and I sweat like a pig

People call me names when they see me
around town

Hiya Spastic!

so cruel
so mean

best to ignore them
but I still hurt deep down

Rollator Blues

This contraption has taken over from my legs

No dancing the night away
No boogie shuffling left to do

My feet follow this damn rollator wherever I go

The four wheels keep going round and round
giving me false hope of independence

I wish I could pick it up and throw it into the
empty void

I am still determined to walk without this piece
of junk

Watch me go and never give up.

Boring

Boring, boring
I don't know what to do
no projects to finish
no people to meet
just shut up
no smiles
no hugging
no sitting down
not what you think
I know but well, what else

ahh! I do like looking at the scenery and the
seaside

Staying at home is just total crap
I feel a prisoner in this world of COVID-19
My brain is very tired and I can't cope with the
new normal
I get frustrated
I feel trapped
with every move I make

The Mask

This mask of a crazy world has no use for me

Eating lunch time paninis, difficult with a cuppa tea

Breathing becomes more like hard work, I have asthma you see

Talking through this mouth-stopping guard is stupid I think you will agree

When will life get back to normal? There's no guarantee

Help me be independent in this unbalanced society.

Ice Cream

How much I like Ice cream
I've missed the soft vanilla with a crumbly flake
and the mint choc chip is just heaven
Salted caramel is lovely too

The taste of ice cream melts away the thoughts
of lockdown

I hope we don't have a third wave
What is the seaside without ice cream?

21

Gone

The mask has gone
I can breathe easier

People look at me like a criminal
They don't get it
I have asthma and other hidden disabilities
but they still judge me

Some shops still won't let me in
It's not fair
My exemption badge is real
Some people don't realize how I feel

Freedom Day

I've missed you so much.
lockdown hid you away from
the hustle and bustle of life

People talking and laughing
all disappeared over night

Coffee shops stood still
human contact stopped in its tracks

until now

It's good to be back
I want to hug you Carmarthen Town
and sing in your streets
                    on Freedom Day

Hooray!

Lockdown is ending
the cafes are open
hooray, hooray

My first drink since last year
oh! it's bliss to be out with other people

Being on my own wasn't very nice
I am so glad
to see my friends once more

27

Part 2
2021

Signs

I can't even understand these signs
English, Welsh and Braille

social distancing
so confusing

I'm not being funny
how can I stay two metres apart from my
support worker?

Fed up and feeling exhausted
I just want life to go back to normal

Cadw pellter cymdeithasol

Cadwch bellter o 2 fetr rhyngoch chi ac eraill.

Social distancing

Please keep a 2m distance between yourself and others.

Pellter o 2 fetr
2 Metre distance

Neges hylendid am y coronafeirws

Ni fydd y toiledau hyn yn cael eu staffio na'u glanhau ar ôl pob defnyddiwr. Byddwch yn ymwybodoleich bod yn defnyddio'r cyfleusterau hyn ar eich risg eich hun.

Coronavirus hygiene notice

These toilets will not be staffed or cleaned after every user. Please be aware that you use these facilities at your own risk.

No Social Distancing

The two-metre rule has finished

Hooray

No social distancing to worry about
People don't shout at me anymore

My arms spread out wide
all the confusion gone

I feel happy to walk around the town again
without fear and blame.

Superhero Triathlon

I feel alive when I become a superhero king

        Every step
                every move I make
                      I make a difference

raising money for good causes
        for people less fortunate than me.

Triathlon inspires me to go all the way
                            to the end

        and give something back
                to people who need help
                      from amazing carers

Fed Up

The clocks have gone back and winter is just
around the corner

Another lockdown might be approaching and I
feel like screaming.

More restrictions again I wonder if Christmas
will go ahead

I'm fed up

I hope 2022 will be better than 2021

I have already lost someone close to me this
year

I need a holiday.
I want to get away
and have time to myself

I can't wait until the summer comes back.

Latte on a Cold Day

A warm latte on a cold day
what more can one ask for?

I wonder how long it will last before
lockdown restrictions forces me
to drink coffee in the car again

I feel my freedom slipping away
I feel trapped and
    I just don't know what to do

  I hate this Covid

  when will it all end?

Mum

I miss my mum so much

She passed away in September

I didn't get to see her during lockdown

Covid stopped me from seeing her

and now she's gone

but mum you are with me
every day in my heart
and I love you so much

Good night and sleep tight

Goodbye Everybody

My journey has come to an end
at mumbles pier

I remember writing my first story here
back in July 2020

and I have really enjoyed every moment of it

Thank you so much to my support worker for
helping me tell my story
through the pandemic

Lockdown wasn't all bad

Goodbye for now

43

Arron Waters

Originally from further West Wales Arron now lives in Carmarthen Town. He is quite obviously a fan of ice -cream, but among his other passions are dancing and a love of animals. There are regular visits to one of his favourite places, Folly Farm. Arron is a member of *The Tywi Salmons* and has competed on behalf of the group at several swimming galas.

Stephen Treharne

Stephen also lives in Carmarthen although he has roots in the Llanddarog area of the county. Stephen has worked for Cartrefi Cymru for nearly five year. Prior to this, for a long time he made his living as a professional chef including spending five years working in Nantes in France. He has also entertained royalty, once cooking for the Duke and Duchess of Kent

Rydyn ni'n adeiladu dyfodol lle mae'r bobl rydyn ni'n eu cefnogi, a'u teuluoedd yn mwynhau bywydau da fel cyfranwyr gwerthfawr i'w cymunedau.

We are building a future where the people we support, and their families enjoy good lives as valued contributors to their communities.

cartrefi cymru
co-operative

Cefnogi Pobl a Chymunedau | Supporting People and Communities